THE BIG GREEN POETRY MACHINE

Our Poetic World

Edited By Donna Samworth

First published in Great Britain in 2023 by:

Young Writers
Remus House
Coltsfoot Drive
Peterborough
PE2 9BF
Telephone: 01733 890066
Website: www.youngwriters.co.uk

All Rights Reserved
Book Design by Ashley Janson
© Copyright Contributors 2023
Softback ISBN 978-1-80459-572-5

Printed and bound in the UK by BookPrintingUK
Website: www.bookprintinguk.com
YB0542LZ

FOREWORD

Welcome Reader,

For Young Writers' latest competition The Big Green Poetry Machine, we asked primary school pupils to craft a poem about the world. From nature and environmental issues to exploring their own habitats or those of others around the globe, it provided pupils with the opportunity to share their thoughts and feelings about the world around them.

Here at Young Writers our aim is to encourage creativity in children and to inspire a love of the written word, so it's great to get such an amazing response, with some absolutely fantastic poems. It's important for children to be aware of the world around them and some of the issues we face, but also to celebrate what makes it great! This competition allowed them to express their hopes and fears or simply write about their favourite things. The Big Green Poetry Machine gave them the power of words and the result is a wonderful collection of inspirational and moving poems in a variety of poetic styles.

I'd like to congratulate all the young poets in this anthology; I hope this inspires them to continue with their creative writing.

CONTENTS

Blackboys Church Of England Primary School, Blackboys

Harrison Brodie (9)	1
Evie Colegate (6)	2
Delilah Neilson (9)	4
Maisie Mulcahy (10)	5
Emilia Briscall (8)	6
Hattie Dunbar (9)	7
Lorenzo Malagoni (6)	8
Jessica Passey (6)	9
Benjy Cottingham (8)	10
Mya Pitt	11
Alice Passey (8)	12
Ginny Lancaster (6)	13
Elodie Dixon (7)	14
Gabi Pollitt (7)	15
Jessica Raphael Hall (7)	16
Phoebe Dixon (9)	17
Bertie Fieldhouse (7)	18
Keegan Jenkins (6)	19
Aggie Thompson (6)	20

Bordesley Village Primary School, Bordesley Village

Ahmed Ibrahim (8)	21
Ismaeel Nasir Uddin (9)	22
Insia Zahra (9)	23
Rimsha Zia (11)	24
Minhazur Rahman (10)	25
Salman Shukri Mohamed (11)	26
Subhayan Manna (8)	27
Aron Samir (11)	28
Alfie Gardner (10)	29
Noorhanis Sofea Mohammad Effendi (9)	30
Eliza Jannat (10)	31
Lailah Dowd (10)	32
Aaliyah Sufi (10)	33
Fatima Abubakar (11)	34
Aadil Waheed (11)	35
Isra Abdi (11)	36

Endon Hall Primary School, Endon

Eleanor Tallentire (6)	37
Oakley John Spencer (7)	38
Annabelle Lymer (7)	39
Hugo Plant (6)	40
Isabelle Munden (6)	41
Mila Gerashi (7)	42
Zarah Khan (6)	43
Isaac Worrall (6)	44

Forest Oak School, Smiths Wood

Serenity Whyte (11)	45
Leighton Craig (11)	46
Alex Merritt (11)	47
Eden Carter (12)	48
Leo Hicks (10)	49
Theo Knox (11)	50
Tyler Horsley (12)	51
Scarlett Thomas (11)	52
Oliver Mills (12)	53
Laina Falle (11)	54
Kim Barnes (10)	55
Aaliyah Gourlay (10)	56
Tianna Randell (10)	57

Danyal Tilling (9)	58
Edward Tozer (10)	59
Alexander O'Neill (9)	60
Lexie Leigh Demaine (12)	61
Arren Cadby (11)	62

Hill View Junior Academy, Sunderland

Emily Furness (10)	63
Alice Young (9)	64
Ruby Richardson (9)	65
Seren Howells (8)	66
Lucy Young (9)	67
Ivy Royal (9)	68
Arabella Howatson (9) & Darcey Williams (8)	69
James O'Donnell (10)	70
Brodie McGlen (9)	71
Holly Hargrave (10)	72
Freya Philliskirk (9)	73
Ethan Brown (9)	74
Elsie Williams (8)	75
Neve Wade (9)	76
Annabelle Evans (10)	77
Tanisha Hussain (8)	78

St Mary's Church of England (Voluntary Aided) Primary School, Swanley

Kyryl Antonov (8)	79
Phoebe Bussey (8)	80
Jessica Caseley (8)	82
Alfie Stockley (9)	84
Nehemias Riojas Conde (11)	86
Isabelle Richards (10)	87
Harry Cook (8)	88
Lily Peters (9)	90
Sophia Williams (8)	91
Juliana Bello (10)	92
Lily Luxton (9)	93
Jacob Smith (10)	94
Carter Lee (10)	95

Mason Cox (10)	96
Teddy Webb (11)	97
Alfie-James Powney (10)	98
Catherine Cayford (8)	99
Iyah-Renae Babafemi (8)	100
Sofia Owen-Walby (8)	101
Mackenzie-Rose Campbell (8)	102
Isaiah Buchanan-Banton (9)	103
Myla-Rose Jares (9)	104
Amelia Horne (11)	105
Clarissa Augustus (9)	106
Eliza Schuiling (7)	107
Hollie Cicognani (8)	108
Lilly Dempsey (8)	109
David Adeyinka (7)	110
Scarlett West (9)	111
Daisy Carter (7)	112
Ollie Cook (7)	113
Tiffany Clayton (7)	114
Harvey Canes (8)	115

St Teresa's Catholic Primary School, Parkfields

Tysharna Ndemen (8)	116
Oliver Jones (7)	117
Ahromeekah Chaparadza (8)	118
Joshua Mugabe (7)	119
Gabrielle Martin-Gray (7)	120
Lycia Coates (8)	121
Leila-Lilly Moulder Comrie (8)	122
Laura Wharchol (8)	123
Mercy George (7)	124
Daniel Nar Singh (8)	125
Amber Saddique (7)	126
Sifat Sangha (7)	127
Archie Hodgson (7)	128
Yuvraj Dhaliwal (8)	129
Dilreet Kaur (8)	130
Thebora Wilbert (8)	131
Ay'sha Rivers (7)	132

The Shrubbery School, Walmley

Paynton Donlon (10)	133
Darcey Knowles	134
Harlow Owusu-Ansah (9)	135
Charles Joseph Leighton (10)	136
Georgina Brown (10)	137
Vibha Sivakumar (9)	138
Atharv Sekhsaria	139
Olivia Blount (9)	140
Daanish Ahmed	141
Jude Southall (9)	142
Tobias Amos Willshire (10)	143

Whitehall Junior Community School, Walsall

Liyana Iqbal (7)	144
Zunairah Imran (11)	145
Sajida Akhter (11)	146
Ruby Joanne Hanley (10)	148
Aliza Malek (10)	150
Reyha Rahman (10)	151
Humera Sayf (11)	152
Laiba Chaudhry (11)	153
Aleena Zaynab (10)	154
Anureet Sidhu (10)	155
Nikola Seferyn (11)	156
Maimoona Sajjad (10)	157
Qaylah Esakjee (10)	158
Sofia Mohammed (10)	159
Najiha Awal (7)	160
Zaina Hussain (11)	161

THE POEMS

My Litter-Picking Walk

We see a can floating up,
And wonder whether to pick it up.
We think *nah, it's no big deal*,
Just think about how nature feels!
But we should think:
There's a can floating up,
I had better pick it up.
We should think about how nature feels,
And how it could end up in a calm green field.
I see a crisp packet lying around,
I pick it up off the ground.
I look around and see a big black bin,
And I glimpse an old tuna tin,
And also put that in the big black bin.
I see a group of beautiful horses all in a big herd;
I remember the litter I picked up and think,
The amount of litter here is truly absurd.

Harrison Brodie (9)
Blackboys Church Of England Primary School, Blackboys

I Am A Little Turtle

I am a little turtle,
Swimming in the sea.
I have a hard shell,
Which is big and green.

I swim 20 miles a day,
I am 70 years old or more!
When I am ready,
I'll lay my eggs on the shore.

I am a little turtle,
Swimming in the sea.
Is that a yummy jellyfish?
Whatever could it be?

I go to see what it is,
And now I think I'm stuck!
This thing is caught around me -
Is this just terrible luck?

I am a little turtle,
I can't swim in the sea;

There is plastic and human rubbish,
And I can't get free.

My friends start to push and pull,
They free my shell and legs.
We swim and go home quickly,
Before we end up dead.

I am a little turtle,
Swimming in the sea,
Please be careful where you put your rubbish,
So I can live safe, happy, and free.

Evie Colegate (6)
Blackboys Church Of England Primary School, Blackboys

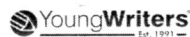

Finding Nature

Do I really want to be trapped inside,
When the light of spring shines through?
I look outside, what a beautiful place,
So I purge myself away
From the claustrophobic air, heavy in my house.
I start running like a cheetah in the wild,
With unique flowers staring at me.
Whimsical whispers of wind flutter through my hair,
As the transparent clouds breathe over me.
My hand sweeps through the emerald leaves,
I feel their life run through my veins.
It brings me joy in my heart and soul,
Whilst I push back all my sadness
That once rushed through my body.
Oh special, spiritual world, please never change.

Delilah Neilson (9)
Blackboys Church Of England Primary School, Blackboys

Our Forest

They're rash, they're hash, they're mean and all,
They cut down our forest of trees standing tall.
They're prioritising money over biodiversity,
We don't stand a chance, they don't even have pity.

They cleared a big space for a new city hall,
They're even installing a swimming pool.
They're ridding us for fields of bright yellow crops,
I'm sure we won't live until the next equinox.

Them and their bulldozers, closer they're coming,
They're heartless, corrupt, cunning.
Then, farewell! The sun shone,
And... *snap!* That's me gone!

Maisie Mulcahy (10)
Blackboys Church Of England Primary School, Blackboys

I Am The World And I Am Crying

I am the world and I am crying,
I'm sad because people are hurting me.
They are cutting down my trees,
They are littering my land,
They are polluting my seas.
The summers are getting hotter,
The winters are getting colder.
Places are flooding,
But nobody seems to care.
Please take good care of me,
I need to be loved.
Help me by:
Driving less and walking more,
Growing more at home,
Looking after my forests and wildlife,
And protecting my land and seas.
If we lived a little greener,
And tried to be a little less meaner,
I would be less sad.

Emilia Briscall (8)
Blackboys Church Of England Primary School, Blackboys

Climate Change

You say you'll fix it and then you don't;
You say you'll do it and then you won't.
I really don't think you understand how I feel about this,
So just hurry up and deal with it.
You know that you're polluting the world,
So stop making my head swirl and twirl.
Your empty words (as Greta Thunberg has said),
Make my head fill with dread.
Honestly, don't you understand
You're making a mess of people's plans.
Don't laugh, don't leave, don't run away;
Make this world a beautiful place.
Can't you just make my day?

Hattie Dunbar (9)
Blackboys Church Of England Primary School, Blackboys

Space Beautiful

How I love space.
Space is unusual, you know?
If you travel through space,
You see lots of planets as you go.
You can see the stars when it's night-time,
Or maybe the space station;
Always floating in space,
Because there's no gravity there.
There is no oxygen or water.
If you did have water, that would be okay,
But if you had a water bottle
That would float away!
Space is beautiful, but be careful:
If you had a dog, it wouldn't stay,
And if you had a sausage,
That would also go away.

Lorenzo Malagoni (6)
Blackboys Church Of England Primary School, Blackboys

The Frog

At the bottom of my garden there is a frog
His friend is a dog
The dog and the frog never scavenge
Because they are well-trained
But one day the dog was ill
They could not go anywhere
The frog frowned and said, "Are you okay?"
"No," said the dog
The frog left the room and worried
I hope the dog is okay
But the dog really wasn't
The frog knew that he wasn't because the dog died
But the frog knew they would still be friends forever.

Jessica Passey (6)
Blackboys Church Of England Primary School, Blackboys

RAF Rescue

The plane was bulging with passengers,
It had never been so full,
People were squashed in corners -
They could hardly move at all.

They were glad to be on the plane,
It was taking them somewhere safe;
To flee the terrifying war
And they were grateful to escape.

The tower called the pilot up:
"Can you make it off the ground
With all the weight and this burning heat?"
"Just watch me," was his response.

Benjy Cottingham (8)
Blackboys Church Of England Primary School, Blackboys

Green Is...

Green is the grass all around my school,
Green is the way we use our recycling rule.

Green are the vegetables Mummy makes me eat,
Green is an apple, crunchy and sweet.

Green is the bottle I refill for shampoo,
Green is me; I hope it's you.

Green are the trees and hedges near me,
Green are the waves on the deep blue sea.

Green is the Earth that belongs to us all,
So let's help the Earth and recycle at school.

Mya Pitt
Blackboys Church Of England Primary School, Blackboys

The Forest

N ight-time owls swoop from tree to tree,
A lert and ready to scatter the deer prick up their ears.
T aking it slow and steady, lolloping around is a cuddly bunny;
U nder the fern leaves sleeping soundly lays a red and brown fox.
R unning around a tree trunk is a cheeky hedgehog.
E ven though they are really tired they don't go to sleep - the animals in the forest go under the trees!

Alice Passey (8)
Blackboys Church Of England Primary School, Blackboys

Plastic Fish

If I had one wish,
I know what it would be:
To remove all the plastic
From the deep blue sea.
Swimming underwater,
What do my two eyes see?
Beautiful fish swimming past me.
But as I look closer,
I see what they really are.
Bottletops and rainbow straws,
And bits of an old toy car.
We are killing our planet
By not being green;
Let's work together
To keep the sea clean.

Ginny Lancaster (6)
Blackboys Church Of England Primary School, Blackboys

The Animal Safari

The tree blows on a safari
Where lots and lots of animals live;
Tigers, cheetahs, leopards and elephants,
Zebras, monkeys, pandas and sloths.
Sloths hang on the trees,
Pandas eat bamboo,
All day the elephants splash water at each other.
A monkey swings through the trees,
Its babies cling to her back.
A bird sings lovely songs.
The hippopotamus cleans
The baby hippopotamus.

Elodie Dixon (7)
Blackboys Church Of England Primary School, Blackboys

Litter Has To Be Gone

Animals are getting sicker
Because of all this litter.
Maybe if this was gone,
Nothing would be wrong.
As I go to school,
People are dropping more;
As I passed a tree
The ground needed me.
I picked up my bag -
The ground looked bad.
So I picked up the litter
With my picker,
So everyone saw me,
And they picked it up with me.
Nothing was the same!

Gabi Pollitt (7)
Blackboys Church Of England Primary School, Blackboys

Nature's Adventure

Cycling through the woods,
On a nature adventure.
Flowers bloom and flowers sing,
And get beautiful every spring.
Horses jumping courses,
Sheep chomping, cows stomping.
I can smell the beautiful blossom on a cherry tree,
I dream of helping the world be green.
No more plastic would be fantastic,
Let's save our beautiful planet,
Nature's Mother Earth.

Jessica Raphael Hall (7)
Blackboys Church Of England Primary School, Blackboys

The Animal Safari

The trees blossomed during the blue sunny day.
The animals ran in the sunlight.
The lions were roaring with pride
As the cubs lay in their Mum's warm, snuggly paws.
The cheetahs ran and the monkeys swung on the trees,
But at night the animals would lie and wait until
The sun rose.
The scary night was as silent as sleep;
Goodnight animals, see you in daylight.

Phoebe Dixon (9)
Blackboys Church Of England Primary School, Blackboys

Sloths

I am a two-toed sloth,
My coat is soft and sable.
My rainforest home is warm and wet.
I love eating leaves,
I sleep many hours a day,
I only go to the toilet once a week
And I move super slow.
I'm scared of harpy eagles,
But more than that: I'm scared of my home being chopped down.

Bertie Fieldhouse (7)
Blackboys Church Of England Primary School, Blackboys

Climate Change

C hanges to the weather,
L ife-threatening to animals,
I ce caps melting,
M ore animals going extinct.
A ffecting the Earth,
T ime to change.
E lectricity saved.

Keegan Jenkins (6)
Blackboys Church Of England Primary School, Blackboys

Rubbish

Rubbish, rubbish
Isn't good.
Plastic, sweet wrappers
In the wood.
Plastic, plastic
Isn't fantastic.

Aggie Thompson (6)
Blackboys Church Of England Primary School, Blackboys

Seasons And The Weather

Winter is like going to Antarctica.
It's freezing, it's snowy,
Also in winter, snowflakes drop down from the sky.
Like Antarctica, it's so cold that the ground turns to slippery ice.

Summer is just as hot as a volcano.
It's boiling.
The ground is like lava
If you step on it, it burns you.
It's so hot that even soil melts.

Spring, the flowers grow faster than ever,
They look nice, like roses.
Flowers get bigger and taller.
The grass gets tall and big like the flowers,
And there's greenery.

Autumn, trees in autumn have more leaves than in winter, spring, and summer,
Because there are more leaves,
It means lots of branches as well.

Ahmed Ibrahim (8)
Bordesley Village Primary School, Bordesley Village

Mankind

The sun is getting warmer, the Earth is turning barren;
The crops are drying as the rivers are rising.
Climate change is taking over like the darkness of night:
Species dying, animals crying,
Floods, drought and fires no longer surprising.
The future looks sullen but it is not too late,
We can befriend the Earth and not make it our fate.
Turn off the lights if you want to see bright;
We can plant more trees to save the bees.
We can recycle and reuse so the Earth is not abused,
We can walk or climb or even glide instead of drive.
We can stop using plastic to make our future fantastic.
Oh, humankind be kind for mankind.

Ismaeel Nasir Uddin (9)
Bordesley Village Primary School, Bordesley Village

Earth In The Wrong Hands

Don't pollute water and air,
Don't throw garbage here and there.
Do not cut trees, never ever!
Search for a solution, stop pollution.
Plant more trees everywhere,
Let us plant them here and there.
Burning fuels causes air pollution;
It's time to embrace a greener solution.
Too many years of human excess
Has put our planet under too much stress.
The first thing to do is to stop deforestation,
A major cause of air pollution.

Insia Zahra (9)
Bordesley Village Primary School, Bordesley Village

Be Part Of The Solution, Not Pollution

Climate change is happening *now*.
Summer is getting hotter,
Heatwaves coming in.
Rainforests suffering from deforestation,
Renewable energy is shrinking.
Oceans are getting trashed,
Hundreds, thousands of animals are in danger.
No more plastic,
And no wore waste,
Because I am fading at a fast pace.
We need life, we need nature,
So, everyone on Planet Earth
Stick with the solution - not the pollution.

Rimsha Zia (11)
Bordesley Village Primary School, Bordesley Village

Pollution

The world is green.
Why can't it be seen?
Because the world isn't clean.
There is pollution.
People are acting like it's exaggerated.
Why can't the birds be heard?
Because people are not spreading the word.
Stop pollution!
Stop the exaggeration.
Why can't we see the sun?
Because we can't go outside and have a run.
Because there is pollution.
Stop pollution!

Minhazur Rahman (10)
Bordesley Village Primary School, Bordesley Village

Ten Years And One Month

I grew up from a seed,
To grow old as a tree.
Forty seasons I survived,
Ten years I withstood.

Spring came at last;
Flowers covered me,
Birds singing happily.
But little did I know,
It was my last spring.

Trees came down, perishing.
These were my only company.
Then came my turn;
They made me burn.
Birds were powerless,
Spring floating away in flames.

Salman Shukri Mohamed (11)
Bordesley Village Primary School, Bordesley Village

Our Planet

O ur Earth is so lively;
U se all its resources lightly.
R ecycle and reuse its resources properly.

P lant more trees regularly,
L ive life happily
A nd protect the nature rationally.
N ature will bless us unconditionally,
E ducating us to keep the environment healthy, eventually
T reating and saving our beloved Earth successfully.

Subhayan Manna (8)
Bordesley Village Primary School, Bordesley Village

Winter

As you feel the wind go by,
A breeze you'll feel on your face.
Be careful; it might go in your eye
And of an icy snowflake you will get a taste.

The cars will drift,
The horse's hooves will crunch.
As soon as you shift,
You'll see a lot more bunch.

If you think that's it,
Be ready for a surprise;
A lot of things happen
As time flies by.

Aron Samir (11)
Bordesley Village Primary School, Bordesley Village

Garden Life

In the garden, it's not just me
Sharing my territory.
Under my feet, light shines:
Time for me to eat.

As I see my delicious feast
Waiting for me, I decide to pounce;
But it scurries under me,
Small, brown and furry.

It runs through a gap,
Away from me.
It's not time for me to eat.
My owners are calling me;
Time to go.

Alfie Gardner (10)
Bordesley Village Primary School, Bordesley Village

Climate Change

Global warming all around;
Causing trouble for the world,
Causing trouble for people.
Please stop climate change.
Stop harming nature,
Reduce pollution, find the solution.
Better use a zero-emission vehicle,
Try walking to work;
Let's save the environment -
How do you feel about it?
Do you want to save the world?
Then welcome to the world.

Noorhanis Sofea Mohammad Effendi (9)
Bordesley Village Primary School, Bordesley Village

Poor Climate!

Every day there's rubbish on the floor,
No one bothering to pick it up.
Not knowing what will happen -
The world is falling apart.

No one's scared about what would happen,
Until they see what will happen.
Life would be duller
Than what they're doing.
It's like the world's life is going.

Eliza Jannat (10)
Bordesley Village Primary School, Bordesley Village

Help

Plants are dying alone,
Whilst we sit at home.

I dread the day they all die,
Because then we won't be able to survive.

Maybe the Earth is doing this to us,
So we must live harmoniously and just.

Plants are dying,
And so are we.

So let's just all be free.

Lailah Dowd (10)
Bordesley Village Primary School, Bordesley Village

Bear

Need to collect my supplies
To hibernate.
Need to catch my prey.
Winter is going to be long,
Need to wait until spring comes.
I'm going to find a nice comfy cave
Need to sleep.
Finally the time has come.
Need to wake up when it's spring
Then the real fun will begin.

Aaliyah Sufi (10)
Bordesley Village Primary School, Bordesley Village

I Wish

Sky filled with smoke,
Not fun when it's every day.
Yesterday it was so fun;
Now it's dark and it hurts.

How can we get out of this?
We don't want to be here.
Every day we go through it again.
I wish it could be better.
I wish,
I wish.

Fatima Abubakar (11)
Bordesley Village Primary School, Bordesley Village

Spider Boy

I am Spider Boy,
I am the unknown;
I never knew until today
When I tried to fly away.
My webs are like no other,
So powerful they can defeat my brother.
Enemies come my way,
But all I do is play.
Remember I am not ordinary:
I am just extraordinary.

Aadil Waheed (11)
Bordesley Village Primary School, Bordesley Village

In The Name Of The Foe

In the name of the foe,
Men fight in war,
Ready to fight the foe.
Gunshots around the world,
Sacrificing themselves for the world,
Standing as their heart is shattered cold.
Happiness used to grow, but not anymore.

Isra Abdi (11)
Bordesley Village Primary School, Bordesley Village

Save The Rainforest

S ave the rainforest
A nimals live there
V isible change is bad
E arth needs rainforests

R ainforests are important for the environment
A nimals there are mostly green
I t is significant to you and me
N ew medicines are found there
F lowers are bright and beautiful
O ne of the greenest places in the world
R ainforests are very warm and wet
E veryone needs to help
S top extinction
T ime to help
S ave the rainforest now.

Eleanor Tallentire (6)
Endon Hall Primary School, Endon

Litter

It is very important to not drop litter
Especially if you are a tiny little critter
It poisons the soil where they stay alive
How do we expect them to survive?
In the ocean, plastic is a huge killer
From turtles to dolphins, it can get stuck in a flipper
We need to think about animals and recycle more
Put litter in the bin and not on the floor.

Oakley John Spencer (7)
Endon Hall Primary School, Endon

Stitch The Dog

My dog loves sleeping,
His name is Stitch the dog.
My dog loves playing,
His name is Stitch the dog.
My dog loves treats,
His name is Stitch the dog.
My dog is so cute,
His name is Stitch the dog.
My dog loves playing football,
His name is Stitch the dog.
I love all the things my dog does.
I love him.

Annabelle Lymer (7)
Endon Hall Primary School, Endon

Wonderful

R ubber tree plants
A mazon river dolphin
I nteresting toucans
N ew flowers growing
F rogs' bright skin
O ver a million species
R aging crocodiles
E quator very hot
S outh America
T all trees.

Hugo Plant (6)
Endon Hall Primary School, Endon

The Seven Seas

Don't drop litter
It could end up in the sea
Be an eco-warrior like me
The ocean has lots of habitats
Big and small
It has orcas and dolphins
And coral that's very tall
Try to recycle where you can
It would be a very good plan.

Isabelle Munden (6)
Endon Hall Primary School, Endon

Nature

N ear and near the sea
A lso, I see a fish
T earing apart a worm
U se a boat to go on the sea
R eally to be helpful
E scape the sharks.

Mila Gerashi (7)
Endon Hall Primary School, Endon

Chubby Cheeks

Chubby cheeks, dimpled chin
And rosy lips with teeth within
Curly hair,
Very fair
Eyes are blue,
Lovely, too
Teacher's pet
Is that you?
Yes, yes, yes!

Zarah Khan (6)
Endon Hall Primary School, Endon

About Animals

I like foxes
I like elephants
They shoot water out of their trunks
Foxes are scary.

Isaac Worrall (6)
Endon Hall Primary School, Endon

Rubbish

Rubbish.
It makes me feel fun-ish.
It's always on the ground,
Then I hear a sound.
I feel like it's someone throwing rubbish.
Then I start to hurry.
There is a boy.
"Oi! What are you doing?"
"I'm throwing rubbish in the bin," he said.
Then he bumped his head.
"That's the sea!"
"Oh... Argh! There's a bee!"
"Oh no, the bee is going to die,
It's stuck in a McDonald's fry!"
"That's not a fry, that's the box.
Quick, before it gets eaten by that fox."
"Throwing rubbish is bad, now I'm really mad."
"Okay, okay, okay, I will throw it in the bin -
I will start off with this plastic tin."
Remember, kids, throwing rubbish is bad...
Recycle it or I will be mad!

Serenity Whyte (11)
Forest Oak School, Smiths Wood

Still Tree

S trong green towering tree
T he tractor is coming towards me
I am staying strong
L ong sturdy branches bobbing in the breeze
L eaves blowing in the strong wind

T ractors driving into us, knocking us down
R oots pulled out of the ground
E vil people getting rid of us
E veryone needs to stop deforestation! *Stop and think!*

Leighton Craig (11)
Forest Oak School, Smiths Wood

The Environment

E arth is being damaged
N ot many people respect it
V ery bad to cut down trees
I worry for the future
R ecycling should happen more
O ur water is dirty
N ature is losing its trees
M any animals are dying
E arth is in danger
N ot enough is being done
T he beaches are full of rubbish.

Alex Merritt (11)
Forest Oak School, Smiths Wood

Stop Killing The Environment

T he salty water
H elps the animals to live
E very day and night

O ceans are beautiful places to be
C lear blue sky with a big shiny sun
E njoy looking at my beautiful waves
A nimals swim under the waves
N ever be afraid to visit the ocean!

Eden Carter (12)
Forest Oak School, Smiths Wood

Recycle

R eusing stuff we don't need
E nergy using wind and solar is good but
C oal and nuclear is bad
Y ou can help nature by recycling
C an you pay attention to nature already?
L ike dumping?
E njoy destroying the planet! Don't... I was being sarcastic!

Leo Hicks (10)
Forest Oak School, Smiths Wood

Wildlife

W ater to keep animals alive
I nterest in saving the trees
L ions roaring through the forests
D eforestation
L isten to the animals cry
I want to protect the animals
F ight for the animals
E verybody fight, let's get it right.

Theo Knox (11)
Forest Oak School, Smiths Wood

Save Our Oceans

People are beginning to realise
That they're doing the wrong thing
By hurting our oceans
Without knowing a single thing
When they throw their rubbish into the sea
More and more fish become endangered
All the rubbish they throw
Is killing the world's ocean population.

Tyler Horsley (12)
Forest Oak School, Smiths Wood

Our Planet

O ur planet
U s it looks after
R eally, we should look after our planet

P lease recycle
L ook after our animals and trees
A nd our seas
N eed to care
E arth is important
T ogether we can make a difference.

Scarlett Thomas (11)
Forest Oak School, Smiths Wood

Leave The Trees Alone

Trees are being cut down all around,
The rainforests should be safe and sound.

Put the axes away, it's not right;
If not today, make it tomorrow night!
If we have to, we will fight!

Our trees should be left alone,
I really hope we are not on our own.

Oliver Mills (12)
Forest Oak School, Smiths Wood

Fish And Ocean

Finding peace in the dark sea.
Swimming away from plastic bags,
Having to swim away from suffocating traps.
Rubbish flowing in the ocean, night and day, every day.

Fish are dying, the ocean is tired.
Open your eyes, carefully try,
Take care of the ocean.

Laina Falle (11)
Forest Oak School, Smiths Wood

Recycle Now!

R ecycle plastic bottles
E very plastic can be recycled
C lean up leaves with a broom
Y ou can plant flowers, you
C an plant trees.
L eaving it is not good
E mpty the paper bin to recycle.

Kim Barnes (10)
Forest Oak School, Smiths Wood

Recycle

R euse our jam jars
E mpty our milk bottles
C ollect plastic bottles to reuse
Y ou can save the planet
C an you help us?
L ollipop sticks can be used
E nvironment needs our help.

Aaliyah Gourlay (10)
Forest Oak School, Smiths Wood

Recycle

R ecycle what you can
E arth needs our help
C lean before you bin
Y ou can reuse lots of things
C an you help us?
L ots of animals get hurt
E very little helps.

Tianna Randell (10)
Forest Oak School, Smiths Wood

Recycle

R euse instead of binning
E very little act helps
C lean the seas
Y ou can pick up the rubbish
L akes should not be rubbish bins
E veryone needs to help.

Danyal Tilling (9)
Forest Oak School, Smiths Wood

Recycle

R ecycle plastic
U se the bins
B in it! Bin it!
B e friendly to the environment
I t is messy
S top throwing litter
H elp each other.

Edward Tozer (10)
Forest Oak School, Smiths Wood

Be Healthy!

H ealthy mind
E at healthy food
A ll your bones will be strong
L et's eat healthily
T ime to exercise
H elp others to exercise.

Alexander O'Neill (9)
Forest Oak School, Smiths Wood

The Seas

Stop littering, it's killing the fish.
Plants and fish will go extinct,
So stop and think
Before you sink.
We have a better future.
Stop killing the fish.

Lexie Leigh Demaine (12)
Forest Oak School, Smiths Wood

What Am I?

I am blue
I am big
I have fish
Living in me
Every minute
I have rubbish thrown in me
The rubbish inside of me
Is slowly killing the fish in me.

Arren Cadby (11)
Forest Oak School, Smiths Wood

The Rainforest

The rainforest is very important, it keeps the Earth together,
But did you know without your help it won't be around forever?
It absorbs carbon dioxide and releases oxygen that we depend on to survive;
As well as this, it prevents global warming and grows food and medicine to keep us alive.
Home to millions of animals and plants, some of which we are still to discover.
Well, what can we do? How can we help it to recover?
A few simple things we can change that are easy to introduce:
Reduce your carbon footprint by walking more, turning heating down and switching lights off when not in use.
Look for responsibly sourced products when you are shopping,
Food like beef, soya beans and palm oil you should think about swapping.
Do your bit and pass on this information;
Save the rainforest - it is important for the next generation.

Emily Furness (10)
Hill View Junior Academy, Sunderland

Today And Yesterday

"Mum, what is a polar bear?" my children say to me.
"Well, it was a white bear that lived in the Arctic, you see.
There were also penguins and the Arctic fox, but none of them survived.
As the world was getting warmer, in time, all of them died.
If only you could have seen them, so beautiful and bright.
I wish we hadn't given up, we needed to unite.
If I could go back in time, I'd tell myself to shout:
We really must recycle and stop throwing things out.
Walk, run, skip or jog,
Instead of driving in fumes and fog.
We can all make a difference if we work hard and try:
There is no plan B and we don't want the world to fry!"

Alice Young (9)
Hill View Junior Academy, Sunderland

The Tree's Life

The strong wind blows a heap of leaves;
The leaves hit the faces of the poor trees.
The woodcutters are no use to us.
Our lives are being hurt.
As the trees lie in agony and the humans live in peace,
The world could be more fair to trees.
On the other hand, we need paper and other stuff.
Trees like to be used as paper,
At least they know that some people need them.
for those trees who rot to pieces, we wish them the best.
If someone ever tells you that trees aren't of any use,
Remind them of paper and even oxygen.
Prove them wrong!
Don't cut the trees!

Ruby Richardson (9)
Hill View Junior Academy, Sunderland

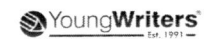

Our Planet

O thers reading this, you help can make an impact on our planet
U nder the circumstances, our planet is going through, we need help
R epeatedly, people don't listen to this message but this time you must

P eople can stop climate change, just listen
L isten, do you like Earth? Then fight for it!
A ll people can make a difference, I admire you
N ow please make a difference
E veryone join in; do a little for a lot
T he people of Earth need to reunite to save our planet.

Seren Howells (8)
Hill View Junior Academy, Sunderland

Ice Murder

In the ocean scene, there's no ice to be seen.
They melted all the ice, they melted everything nice.
Humans have destroyed our habitat, they've made it where it's at.
The community is mad because it is so bad.
As I wonder what lies ahead of me, humans take ice with glee.
Help us, before it's too late; they put life on your plate.
Climate change affects us all, every day, icebergs fall.
Walk to school if you can, much better than a car or van.
You have the chance to save us all, making changes big and small.

Lucy Young (9)
Hill View Junior Academy, Sunderland

I Like...

I like the different colours of the autumn leaves,
That float down from the blossoming trees.
It makes me feel warm and snug;
Except for when there are lots of bugs.

It makes me sad when the sky is grey,
And all I wish for is a bright blue day.
It makes me happy when the flowers bloom,
It's so much better than doom and gloom.
I love it when the grass is fresh and green,
It really helps my football team.

It makes me mad what our amazing world faces,
And all I want is some brand-new changes.

Ivy Royal (9)
Hill View Junior Academy, Sunderland

The Two Polar Bears

One early winter's night,
As the sun shines bright,
As the waves
Splash upon the caves,
As the glowing berries
Shine very merry,
The moon goes away to fade.
As we seek and hide,
He will try to find
Us down the mountainside;
As he tracks us down,
We will follow him around.
As the trees breeze
With their green leaves,
As we dive into the water's waves,
As the bright white snow
Sets on the trees,
Protect the world -
Turn it into
A flaming flare of kindness.

Arabella Howatson (9) & Darcey Williams (8)
Hill View Junior Academy, Sunderland

Yelp For Help!

Rising seas, forest fires, none of this to our desire,
Is Earth beautiful?
Very! But everything is temporary,
Neon leaves upon luscious trees, animals having to plead.
Animals going extinct; all of these things are linked.
Polar bears losing their habitat,
All of their ice going *splat!*
All of this mess and pollution,
Does Greta Thunberg have a solution?
Plant more trees? She agrees.
You too!
You can help!
All you have to do is answer this yelp for help!

James O'Donnell (10)
Hill View Junior Academy, Sunderland

I Am A Tree

I am a tree, tall and strong,
With branches reaching for the sky.
I stand here in this world,
Watching it go by.

I see birds, bees, and butterflies
Buzzing around, day and night.
I see them grow
But the world's in a plight.

I also see the pollution,
The rubbish and the waste.
My branches sag to see the planet
In such a state.

We must all do our part,
To protect and save
Our beautiful planet,
And all that it deserves.

Brodie McGlen (9)
Hill View Junior Academy, Sunderland

What Is Going On Around Me In Nature?

The wind is howling,
The trees are swaying,
The grass is growing;
Smells of roses and daisies fill the air.
Birds are tweeting
From high up in the sky,
The laughter of little children
Such joyful sounds.
The sun shines high
Up in the sky,
Until the great grey moon comes out
And the stars twinkle beside it.
The warm glow mixed
With the breezy air
Feels just like
A fairy tale.

Holly Hargrave (10)
Hill View Junior Academy, Sunderland

Help The World

Stop the pollution, there has to be a solution.
Stop cutting down trees, it makes the world wheeze.
Sea life is in danger from rubbish floating in the waters,
We need to take action on what our schools have taught us.
Whether it's a tin or a can, make sure you put it in the recycling van.
It's nearly time for fun in the sun, so get your walking boots on.
Put the car away and enjoy your summer day.

Freya Philliskirk (9)
Hill View Junior Academy, Sunderland

Life In The Rainforest

A capuchin swings from tree to tree,
Having fun on the vines in the canopy.

The leaves and branches make a big umbrella;
A perfect home for a sloth and a gorilla.

Jaguars and tigers prowl around the forest floor,
They scare the macaws with their loud, fierce roar.

Three million creatures live in the rainforest trees;
It's dark and wet and twenty-eight degrees.

Ethan Brown (9)
Hill View Junior Academy, Sunderland

The Forest

Nature is amazing,
Forests are cool!
Trees make oxygen
You'll learn this in school.

Bees are busy
In the flowers,
Gathering the pollen for hours and hours.

Foxes sniff around,
Looking for their tea,
A flash of red and off they flee.

Roots are on the floor,
So please be aware:
One little trip could give you a scare!

Elsie Williams (8)
Hill View Junior Academy, Sunderland

Fed Up Fish

This is my home, don't you know?
I want to be a fish in the pond, not out!
What is this you throw at me?
Plastic bottles?
Let me help you with that;
Recycle them, that is that!
You can't see me,
My water is too mucky!
Come on! Stop making me so dirty.
Help protect and keep our planet clean,
So little fish like me don't have to dream!

Neve Wade (9)
Hill View Junior Academy, Sunderland

Let Plants Grow

I like watching flowers grow,
Their pretty petals fall down slow.
I love the colours pink and red,
Roses shine brightly above my head.
The sun and rain help the flowers grow,
It makes me smile as I see the river flow.

Annabelle Evans (10)
Hill View Junior Academy, Sunderland

Protect Planet Earth

G rowth,
R ecycle,
E ven the
E nvironment;
N ever forget that.

Tanisha Hussain (8)
Hill View Junior Academy, Sunderland

Please Help Me!

I flow around the Earth,
I get poisoned every day!
People don't care about me, people destroy me.
All of my animals becoming extinct,
All of the living creatures becoming extinct.

We are rivers; we can feel, we can see,
We feel when you pollute us.
We call for help! We call for help!
But people don't hear what we say!

Lots of fires around the globe,
People take water from me, to put them out.
I want to put them out but as the people take water from me,
I deteriorate and then I die.

I flow as fast as I can to wash the rubbish away,
But it doesn't work.
Please help me, save me, please get the plastic away from me.
I want to ask you a question:
Do you want to save me... or not?

Kyryl Antonov (8)
St Mary's Church of England (Voluntary Aided) Primary School, Swanley

The Planet

Careless people dumping rubbish in my ocean blue,
Pushing and shoving, trying to escape from the contaminated land.
Waves howling like a lonesome wolf,
Water of life flowing through my mind.

Oceans and streams howling in pain
As vehicles dump rubbish red and black.
Salty sea not so salty any more, as gutters blow out waste.
Plastic strangling whoever dares to take a bite
Rubbish flowing through my mind as fish die with sadness.

Why don't they care, why don't they see the pain I feel?
Trying to hold back my sadness as my sea friends die.
I choose to stay strong, but at what cost?
Those monsters on land, they don't care -
They dump rubbish into my blue sea.

I know I drown people, I know I kill,
But people are bad and people are good.
They destroy my people and my ocean blue.
The salty sea, not so salty anymore,
Turns to dust and stars fade away.
Trees dying from the rubbish galore,
As those monsters sit and enjoy the show.

Phoebe Bussey (8)
St Mary's Church of England (Voluntary Aided) Primary School, Swanley

Our Planet

I get trash thrown in me by careless people.
I flow all day, but people always get in the way.
I save the Earth, but people don't save me;
Do people care about me?
Save the Earth!
Animals stuck in trash!
Save the Earth!
No one cares, but they really should...
We need to change the world!
People are getting hurt.
Save the Earth!

I'm angry at the careless people.
I'm sorry for all the animals that are suffering.
Why don't they love me?
People swim in me, not caring.
Save our world!
Help us to make this world a better place.
Save our world!
It's a disaster! Help Earth now!
I beg you,

We all need your help!
Save our world!

I cry all day... no one hears,
No one cares.
I'm sad all day.

Jessica Caseley (8)
St Mary's Church of England (Voluntary Aided) Primary School, Swanley

The Planet

I flow around the globe
As fast as a racing car,
Pollution I get every day,
I get rubbish in me.

Smells like cold wind,
Smells like rubbish in me,
Smells flowing inside me.
Pollution flowing in my water.

I feel like pollution is inside me,
I feel like cold weather is coming to me.
I don't like rubbish in my water.
I can see and hear but no one knows.

I am an ocean; just water, but I have feelings.
I can see and also hear, they can't see me but I'm here.
I am just a river or a lake,
Just peace and calm.

I can hear sounds and noises,
I just want to escape this.

I hate just being water,
I need to escape this.
I can talk but nobody knows,
I just want to be free today.

Alfie Stockley (9)
St Mary's Church of England (Voluntary Aided) Primary School, Swanley

Mountain Environment

M any people say, spending money in the shops will help the local area
O utrageous weather, never-ending
U p high in the mountains, you will see animals
N ever drop litter; it affects the environment
T oo much traffic could affect the air

S now is on the edges of the top of the mountain
N ature helps animals adapt to the mountain
O ther people say, too many tourists could erode the mountain's soil
W eather could affect people's breathing
D oes litter help the environment? *No!*
O n the one hand, people don't care about the mountain's environment by littering
N ever drop litter!

Nehemias Riojas Conde (11)
St Mary's Church of England (Voluntary Aided) Primary School, Swanley

Mountain Nature

M ountain environments
O utstanding sights
U nusual animals
N ature, nature, nature
T o adapt you must learn
A nimals are important
I nside and outside, they are as important as you
N ever drop litter; it affects the environment.

A re you aware?
N o animal should be extinct
I n rocky mountainous areas, plants grow in amazing places
M ountain goats, Himalayan pandas, rhinos and deer
A nimals are as important as you
L ove and respect animals
S ave, save, save the environment!

Isabelle Richards (10)
St Mary's Church of England (Voluntary Aided) Primary School, Swanley

The Planet

Trees burning across the world,
As bright as a firework.
Pollution is practically everywhere,
Extreme fires destroy the environment.

Volcanoes bursting open;
Climate change is happening.
Choking fire spreading quickly,
Fire burning trees so fastly.

Animals are getting hurt by the fire,
Every day, trees are dying.
Plants are dying,
Save the environment!

Fire spreading as we speak,
Protect the trees!
Fire destroying businesses,
Fire as strong as the Hulk.

Heatwaves causing climate change,
Flames as hot as the sun.

Flames spreading as the night comes by -
I'm sorry for what we've done.

Harry Cook (8)
St Mary's Church of England (Voluntary Aided) Primary School, Swanley

Our Planet

I flow around the Earth
With plastic all over me.
I'm as fast as light;
Why am I getting polluted?
All of my friends are getting hurt:
Do people like me?
Why do they want to destroy me?
Please, do not throw rubbish in me.
My best friend is getting killed;
My whale, please save them, not kill them.
The environment is going to get worse and worse.
It's your fault!
Do you want to hurt me?
Help me! Do you want a beach or not?
Imagine how clean the sea would be if...
I did not get polluted!
I don't think anyone likes me.

Lily Peters (9)
St Mary's Church of England (Voluntary Aided) Primary School, Swanley

The Planet

Protect the water; without it, no beach for you,
As splashy as a kicking baby.
I'm being polluted every day,
Nearly all the time, I'm dying.

Don't pollute me, please, I beg you;
I don't really deserve it.
Everyone does something wrong.

Help me, I'm fading away.
Everybody needs to help.
Light doesn't exist to me any more,
People don't care about me.

Hope I live another day,
Only my friends are the things I care about,
Pollution is bad, rethink your actions;
Every animal is endangered.

Sophia Williams (8)
St Mary's Church of England (Voluntary Aided) Primary School, Swanley

Save Our Planet

R ecycle the universe
E nd the littering
C lean the world
Y oung love
C lean the environment
L ove our planet
E nvironment needs nature

Don't litter,
Keep the world safe.
Clean our planet,
Love our eco-system.
Put all rubbish in the bin,
Keep nature on our planet.
Don't put the world in danger,
Keep everyone safe.
If nature keeps us, we keep nature.
Never, ever put rubbish in the sea.
Help the animals.
Keep ourselves tidy and kind.

Juliana Bello (10)
St Mary's Church of England (Voluntary Aided) Primary School, Swanley

Our Planet

S ave yourself and others
A lways bin litter sensibly
F ires are not allowed
E verything should be clean

E nergy is good for you
N ature is part of a good environment
V ulnerable animals are in danger
I t's important to the world
R ecycle everything
O xygen helps
N o danger
M ore happiness
E njoy the fresh air
N o littering
T rees should not be cut down.

Lily Luxton (9)
St Mary's Church of England (Voluntary Aided) Primary School, Swanley

Mountain Environments

M agical views
O ustanding beauty
U nused train (only for bad weather)
N ever drop litter - it's bad for the environment
T raffic pollutes the air

S now up above
N ature down below
O n the snow, there's a guanaco
W ork provided down below
D on't cause erosion
O ur environment has changed
N ever take the train (you should walk so you get healthy).

Jacob Smith (10)
St Mary's Church of England (Voluntary Aided) Primary School, Swanley

Carbon Footprint

C onserve energy
A marvellous planet
R ecycle your rubbish
B in your litter
O ur planet
N ow we can save our planet

F ire causes pollution
O ur oceans are dying
O ur choice
T rees should not be cut down
P ollution can kill
R ubbish is destroying our planet
I nterfere and help
N o littering
T ime to spread the word!

Carter Lee (10)
St Mary's Church of England (Voluntary Aided) Primary School, Swanley

Nature

M any people climb up the mountain
O utstanding views
U nusual weather
N ature, nature, nature
T raffic, traffic, traffic

S ave it from pollution
N ever litter
O nly throw litter in the bin
W hirlwind
D on't go on the train
O xygen as scarce as a bear
N ature helps animals adapt to the mountain.

Mason Cox (10)
St Mary's Church of England (Voluntary Aided) Primary School, Swanley

Mountain Environments

B e better; don't litter
E xciting, breathtaking views, as majestic as nature
N ever be heartless and pollute the area by car

N ever, never, never make the mountains cry
E ven traffic pollutes the area
V isit Ben Nevis
I can help by not going in a car
S o save the environment and nature won't be destroyed.

Teddy Webb (11)
St Mary's Church of England (Voluntary Aided) Primary School, Swanley

The Environment

E nd littering
N ever trash the environment
V ile litter spilling
I n years the world will be a better place
R eject littering
O h, we try to help
N ever give up
M ake the world a better place
E nd harm to the environment
N ever stop helping
T he amount of litter is as big as the moon.

Alfie-James Powney (10)
St Mary's Church of England (Voluntary Aided) Primary School, Swanley

The Planet

I flow and flow above the cold water,
It is not good.
I run and run like a cheetah.
I'm as blue as the sky,
I'm everywhere.
I surround the ground.
Everyone throws rubbish in me.
Does no one care about me?
Do you know I'm water?
Animals live inside of me -
You're polluting me and killing them,
The animals that live in the ocean.

Catherine Cayford (8)
St Mary's Church of England (Voluntary Aided) Primary School, Swanley

Inside The Rainforest

Animals roam Earth; we follow them
Like we follow God.
Sharks swim through the blue,
Sea octopuses swim through the cold seaweed.
A beautiful world of wonder.
Out of the sea, on land,
Is a furry baby panda, finding bamboo.
As the cloudy blue sky sets,
We walk in the rainforest.
As the pink cotton candy sky appears,
Our Earth is an amazing place.

Iyah-Renae Babafemi (8)
St Mary's Church of England (Voluntary Aided) Primary School, Swanley

Our Earth Is There For You

O ur Earth is beautiful;
U nder the blue sky lie fantastic creatures.
R ead the amazing books.

P lease stop polluting the Earth,
L and is greater than the sea,
A nd outstanding creatures God has made.
N o more pollution,
E nclosures for helpless animals.
T he ocean is calm forever.

Sofia Owen-Walby (8)
St Mary's Church of England (Voluntary Aided) Primary School, Swanley

The World Of Insects

Over the hills, birds chirp high;
Here comes a little butterfly,
Flying high on the trees.
Little insects munch little berries,
Then they will go in their little homes.
It's their time to go.
Now the birds start to chirp low,
Over the hills, so now you know;
It's time for us to go home.
Goodbye, see you next time.

Mackenzie-Rose Campbell (8)
St Mary's Church of England (Voluntary Aided) Primary School, Swanley

The Planet

I blow through the trees,
Thinking am I wrong?
As strong as an armadillo,
I sometimes rip up trees.
Hitting animals like a flying saucer.
I sometimes make tsunamis,
Killing innocent people.
I am sorry for what I've done.
Why does it have to be this way?
I only want peace.

Isaiah Buchanan-Banton (9)
St Mary's Church of England (Voluntary Aided) Primary School, Swanley

Save The Environment

E nergy is running out
N ature
V ulnerable
I enjoy life
R ecycle more
O ur world needs to stay clean
N o littering
M ore happiness
E nergy
N ature is getting destroyed
T hankful for our world.

Myla-Rose Jares (9)
St Mary's Church of England (Voluntary Aided) Primary School, Swanley

Nature!

N ever litter: it can harm animals
A lways carry your rubbish up the mountain
T rees are outstanding but are getting chopped down
U nderstand that animals have feelings
R ecycle your litter to help the Earth
E nvironments need your help.

Amelia Horne (11)
St Mary's Church of England (Voluntary Aided) Primary School, Swanley

Save Our Planet

R ecycle things that you don't need
E lectricity can be used less often
C are for your world
Y our planet needs to be saved
C lean up litter
L ittering is wrong
E co-friendly life.

Clarissa Augustus (9)
St Mary's Church of England (Voluntary Aided) Primary School, Swanley

I Am

I am the water that you swim in.
I am the sea you play with.
I am the sand you use to create things.
I am the sun that glows.
I am the leaves that blow off the trees.
I am the sun that shines bright in the morning.

Eliza Schuiling (7)
St Mary's Church of England (Voluntary Aided) Primary School, Swanley

Earth Animals

I am the fluffy panda eating bamboo.
I am the pig running for safety.
I am the cute cat that destroys everything.
I am the dog that barks so loud.
I am the lion relaxing on the throne.

Hollie Cicognani (8)
St Mary's Church of England (Voluntary Aided) Primary School, Swanley

The Good Panda

I can feel the breeze on my fluff,
Eating bamboo in the rising sun.
But no one can catch me
When I run in the sun.
I am a herbivore
That eats plants all day
And never stops.

Lilly Dempsey (8)
St Mary's Church of England (Voluntary Aided) Primary School, Swanley

Things And Animals

I am the delicious sweets on a shiny red table.
I am the scary, speedy animals.
I am the country you live in.
I am the people that take care of children,
I am the queen and the king.

David Adeyinka (7)
St Mary's Church of England (Voluntary Aided) Primary School, Swanley

Save Our Seas

Clean our planet and seas.
Stop littering, don't put rubbish in the sea.
Don't pick out weeds from the sand,
Save our kind and lovely sea animals.
Please join Team Sea.

Scarlett West (9)
St Mary's Church of England (Voluntary Aided) Primary School, Swanley

The Seas

I smell the salt in the sea,
I see the ocean's crashing waves.
I hear the ocean birds screeching,
I touch the sand on the ground.
I taste the sand all around.

Daisy Carter (7)
St Mary's Church of England (Voluntary Aided) Primary School, Swanley

Nature I Am

I am the nature that grows more and more,
I am the sun that keeps it going.
I am the flower that grows from the ground;
I am the nature that keeps you alive.

Ollie Cook (7)
St Mary's Church of England (Voluntary Aided) Primary School, Swanley

Earth

E ducational
A mazing nature
R ed leaves
T icklish branches
H uge forests.

Tiffany Clayton (7)
St Mary's Church of England (Voluntary Aided) Primary School, Swanley

Cats

Cats scratch sofas.
Cats go meow.
Cats are cute.
I love you cats.

Harvey Canes (8)
St Mary's Church of England (Voluntary Aided) Primary School, Swanley

Please Save The World

Please save the world.
Keep us all safe from things that don't belong to you,
And never throw rubbish on the floor.

Please save the world.
We have to keep rubbish in our pockets until we reach our destination.
Put it in the bin when you don't need it, so the animals
Don't die in the sea or where they live.

Please save the world.
Leave the animals alone and help
To save the world.

Please save the world.
We all have to look after the world, so stop
Being ever so rude.
Stop dreaming, wake up and do it.

Tysharna Ndemen (8)
St Teresa's Catholic Primary School, Parkfields

Help The Environment, Please

Help the environment, please!
We need help,
So you can help us by not littering.

Help the environment, please!
The environment is not clean,
So can you make it more green?
Please don't be mean,
Or you will have to help us clean.

Help the environment, please!
It is not clean.
If you pick up plastic, you are fantastic,
If you drop litter, you will make me bitter,
If you make pollution, I will find a solution.

Oliver Jones (7)
St Teresa's Catholic Primary School, Parkfields

Saving The Ocean From Litter

Save the ocean from litter,
Else it will make me bitter.

Save the ocean because if you drop trash,
It will splash.
You will be leaving the ocean dirty
And killing the animals with litter.

Save the ocean because if you keep on doing harm,
It won't be calm.

Save the ocean because if you keep on trashing the sea,
It will damage me.

Save the ocean for all to see,
And let it be.

Ahromeekah Chaparadza (8)
St Teresa's Catholic Primary School, Parkfields

What Can You Do?

Please be kind and don't dirty our sea,
The whales need clean water and food.

What can you do?
Please don't drop trash because it will clash with the fish and whales.

What can you do?
Please stop dropping your nets so the birds can be free.
If you don't, they won't be free.

What can you do?
If you see trash, don't just stand there:
Think of a solution.

Joshua Mugabe (7)
St Teresa's Catholic Primary School, Parkfields

Leave The Nature Alone Please!

The green nature grows,
All the trees stand still,
So don't be mean
And cut the green trees.

Leave nature alone, please!
God saved the glorious green;
So don't be mean
And make a bad scene.

Leave nature alone, please!
Stop cutting down the trees;
They do no harm to you,
But you do harm to trees.

Save our planet now,
So we can take a bow.

Gabrielle Martin-Gray (7)
St Teresa's Catholic Primary School, Parkfields

How Can You Help Animals?

How can you help animals?
If you see rubbish in the beautiful sea,
Make sure to give it a clean
Or you'll be mean.

How can you help animals?
If you see fleas on a dirty cat,
Don't just sit there drinking cans of pop:
Clean the cat on the mat.

How can you help animals?
If you see rubbish trapping the fish,
Make sure to set it free
On a little dish.

Lycia Coates (8)
St Teresa's Catholic Primary School, Parkfields

Helping The Environment

Helping the environment is a good thing to do;
Helping the environment keeps the place blue.

Plastic is not fantastic,
And the sea is full of elastic.
Clean our world with a super magnet!

Please don't litter,
Or I will get bitter!

The Earth has guilt,
The sea is built.

Please keep this place safe,
Or our world will be a dangerous place.

Leila-Lilly Moulder Comrie (8)
St Teresa's Catholic Primary School, Parkfields

What Can You Do?

What can you do?
If you see a lot of pollution,
Remember, there is always a solution.

What can you do?
If you see a can in the sea,
Where else could it be?

What can you do?
Make sure you keep our planet green,
Or else it will turn into a bad scene.

What can you do?
Make sure you pick up all your litter,
So you don't hurt a little critter.

Laura Wharchol (8)
St Teresa's Catholic Primary School, Parkfields

Leave The Beautiful Whales Alone

Leave the beautiful whales alone!
We need them in our sea.
They swim in our beautiful ocean,
So beautiful as can be.

Leave the beautiful whales alone!
We need them in our world,
They swim calmly in the beautiful ocean.

Leave the beautiful whales alone!
We need them on our happy Earth.
They swim in our peaceful ocean,
They mean no harm.

Mercy George (7)
St Teresa's Catholic Primary School, Parkfields

Leave The Whales Alone, Please

Leave the whales alone, please.
We need water for the sea.
They swim in the ocean,
Let them be.

Leave the whales alone, please.
We need them in our sea;
They are our friends -
Let them be.

Leave the whales alone, please.
They are graceful and calm,
They are friendly and nice.
Let them survive.

Daniel Nar Singh (8)
St Teresa's Catholic Primary School, Parkfields

Leave The Whales Alone, Please!

Leave the whales alone, please!
They are graceful and happy for you.
Please leave them;
They don't want to harm you.

Leave the whales alone, please!
They are sweet and kind,
They will not hurt you.

Leave the whales alone, please!
They are the best blue sea animals.

Amber Saddique (7)
St Teresa's Catholic Primary School, Parkfields

What Can You See?

What can you see?
If you see litter
And don't pick it up,
You are harming
The environment.

If you see pollution,
Don't just stand there -
There is a solution.

What can you see?
If you see plastic on the ground,
Remember, plastic isn't fantastic.

Sifat Sangha (7)
St Teresa's Catholic Primary School, Parkfields

Save The Whales

Please don't drop rubbish into the sea,
You are spoiling it for me.
Please don't drop cans in the sea;
Let the animals be free.

Please don't drop rubbish in the sea,
You are spoiling it for the whales.
Let them be free in the deep blue sea.

Archie Hodgson (7)
St Teresa's Catholic Primary School, Parkfields

Nature

Leave nature
As it will set you free.
Leave nature,
Do what you can,
Help nature be free.
Leave nature,
Believe in nature,
Do what you can,
Leave nature green.
Leave nature
As clean as you can
Let nature gleam.

Yuvraj Dhaliwal (8)
St Teresa's Catholic Primary School, Parkfields

Save The World

Save the world.
When you see some pollution,
You feel it piling up,
There's always a solution.

Save the world.
If you recycle plastic,
And everyone sees,
They'll call you fantastic.

Dilreet Kaur (8)
St Teresa's Catholic Primary School, Parkfields

Our Planet Is Nice And Clean

Let the planet be nice and green,
Let's all try to keep the planet clean.
Keep the rubbish in the bin please,
Help the planet look good.
Helping to heal our natural planet,
To make a happy planet!

Thebora Wilbert (8)
St Teresa's Catholic Primary School, Parkfields

What Will You See?

What will you make?
What will you do?
Let the animals be free -
Plastic is not fantastic.

Let the whales be free
In the deep blue sea.
They are kind to me.

Ay'sha Rivers (7)
St Teresa's Catholic Primary School, Parkfields

The Earth Needs Help

"Help!" shouts the Earth. "Someone's turned up the oven!"
"Help!" screams the Earth. "Someone's left the bath running!"
"Help!" squeaks the Earth. "My ice cream is melting!"
"Help!" shrieks the Earth. "I'm choking on the gases!"
"Help!" squawks the Earth. "This plastic coat is tightening!"

"Let's help," said the teacher. "Let's start cycling!"
"Let's help," said the farmer. "Keep the wind turbines turning and the solar power flowing!"
"Let's help," said the shopkeeper. "Let's keep on planting!"
"Let's help," said the doctor. "Make sure we keep recycling!"

"Thank you," sang the Earth, "for protecting me from global warming!"

Paynton Donlon (10)
The Shrubbery School, Walmley

Sustainability Rules

S ummer's gone and winter's here, but can you really tell?
U nusually warm weather can make winter hot as hell
S o climate change is really here, it is a real thing
T ake a chance or do nothing, the birds will no longer sing
A nother chance for us all to help the planet
I n Davos, world leaders will hopefully plan it
N ow we can all do our bit
A nd stop rubbish going in a landfill pit
B uy less things and recycle more
L earn to help, and help some more
E arth needs our help now, doing nothing is unacceptable.

Darcey Knowles
The Shrubbery School, Walmley

The African Elephant

Deep in the jungle where the animals play.
Lives a beautiful elephant playing all day.
He's as big as a house, but scared of a mouse,
And just wants to keep his family about.
Extinction is near, and so we all fear,
That elephants will be no more.
So, if we want elephants to stay alive
Then humans will have to pay the price.
Please do not kill our wildlife, it is SO wrong:
Remember these words like you'd remember a song.

Harlow Owusu-Ansah (9)
The Shrubbery School, Walmley

Rainforests

R ainforests are huge
A nd the animals rule
I nsects in colonies and groups
N ature is thriving everywhere you look
F inding different animals playing around
O ver the trees and bushes and wildflowers
R espect and protect our rainforests
E verything is unique and different
S uper large trees to shelter animals in the rain
T hat are different sizes.

Charles Joseph Leighton (10)
The Shrubbery School, Walmley

The Rainbow

This rainbow is magical,
This rainbow is kind,
This rainbow I know of
Is actually mine!

This rainbow is beautiful,
This rainbow can help,
This rainbow is nature
Helping itself.

The storm has stopped,
The sun has appeared
The rainbow shines through
Everyone's fears.

It will fade, it will go,
We will wait for the next one
To appear with a glow!

Georgina Brown (10)
The Shrubbery School, Walmley

King Of Beasts

I am ferocious,
Humans are atrocious.
They are monstrous,
Whilst some are preposterous.

Antelopes are tasty,
But need to think about their safety.
I hunt for prey,
But they sometimes get away.

I need twenty hours of sleep,
With plenty to eat.
Never sleep with dread;
I go hunting instead.

Save the lions,
Save the environment.

Vibha Sivakumar (9)
The Shrubbery School, Walmley

Why We Recycle

We make sure we **R**ecycle
Because we want th**E** world
To have fuel, so we **C**an protect
The everyone so that **Y**oung
People can realise how they **C**ould recycle
And **L**earn
To be responsible and **E**co-friendly.

Atharv Sekhsaria
The Shrubbery School, Walmley

We Can Change Now!

We can change now by not chopping down our trees!
Stop using plastic things and start recycling things!
The world's in our hands, especially in our dreams,
Because our imagination flows through the leaves.
We cannot leave our world like this,
So please help while we can!

Olivia Blount (9)
The Shrubbery School, Walmley

Long Live The Environment

Recycle recyclables,
Control deforestation,
Supportive environment.
Glorious biodiversity,
Life-saving ozone,
Disastrous pollution.
Suffocating factories.
Terrifying methane,
Treasure greenery,
Embrace solar energy.
Respect habitat.

Daanish Ahmed
The Shrubbery School, Walmley

Green

G lobal warming is a problem
R emember, millions of trees are chopped down
E ssential items are needed for this
E veryone needs to play their part to fight this
N ever forget the Earth needs your help.

Jude Southall (9)
The Shrubbery School, Walmley

The Chip Van

Smelly!
Exhaust fumes in their plumes.
Odour of fat!
I've had enough of that!

Poor little fish,
Go back to the sea!
Just serve a cake with a cup of tea.

Tobias Amos Willshire (10)
The Shrubbery School, Walmley

Don't Litter

D on't litter because it will ruin our beautiful world, when you litter, animals get curled
O ne day when we stop littering our lunch, there will be animals in a bunch
N ever litter because there should be punishments and our world might end
T ell everyone to never ever litter, and put rubbish in the bin

L ittering is bad for the Earth, same with smoking or vaping, animals might be choking
I love this planet, probably other people do as well, so you are ruining it for everyone
T he planet is very special to lots of people, if you litter you are losing the plot
T his planet means so much to people, when you play put your rubbish in the bin
E veryone loves this world, if you don't then get out because this world is full of clout
R abbits, birds, and insects are dying from rubbish: you better not litter because many people like animals, some people even write about them.

Liyana Iqbal (7)
Whitehall Junior Community School, Walsall

Save Our Earth

The Earth we walk upon is crying out in pain;
She complains to us in a melody of rain.
Clouds are filling up the sky,
No more places for the birds to fly.
Look after the Earth, with all your heart -
Every single one of us needs to play a part.
Pick up your litter, switch off your lights,
Recycle your rubbish; this is our fight.
As the ice is melting, the animals have nowhere to live:
The oceans are becoming empty, it's our time to give.
The animals are dying as the climate changes,
The temperature is rising to dangerous ranges.
Mother Earth has given us a lot -
We need to help before she starts to rot!

Zunairah Imran (11)
Whitehall Junior Community School, Walsall

Save Our Environment

We should help the environment in every way
So that we can breathe fresh air every day.
In addition to this, we could plant some trees,
Or remove litter from the seas.
Our environment must be protected;
It should be helped and not neglected,
Otherwise humans and animals might feel dejected.
We must remove rubbish from our plants or they'll die;
As a consequence, they'll be infested with flies.
This is what all humans very much despise.
People should also stop smoking, as this contaminates the air,
Which could likely cause choking, and that is not fair.
The animals and wildlife should not suffer;
So let's care and prevent this further.
Let's take responsibility before animals become extinct:

It makes no difference whether we're animals or humans because we are linked.
Hopefully we'll be the solution to pollution.

Sajida Akhter (11)
Whitehall Junior Community School, Walsall

Recycling And The Environment

Bottles are green,
Cans are blue;
This poem's about littering
And what you can do!
Put the tin
In the bin.
Do it with cardboard too,
Because everyone is watching what you do!
The Earth is our planet,
We must keep it clean.
Put things in the bin
Or the plants will die:
The environment will be bad,
You will have no oxygen
And neither will I!
We'll have no food,
You shouldn't be littering;
That's not the right thing to do.
Please stop littering,

It's ruining our homes
And the Earth's too.
I hope you're listening
Because you shouldn't be littering!

Ruby Joanne Hanley (10)
Whitehall Junior Community School, Walsall

Earth

We all live on Earth.
Our Earth is beautiful and full of plants, flowers, and animals.
The Earth is a part of the solar system.
Our Earth needs help because we have made so much mess.
Stop messing with our Earth!
Stop cutting trees!
Stop eating animals such as chickens, pigs and ducks.
Start helping to protect plants and trees,
Start giving water and saving plants.
Our Earth needs help,
Our Earth is crying.
If we do these things our Earth will last.
Save Earth, save life.

Aliza Malek (10)
Whitehall Junior Community School, Walsall

Help The Environment

Life changes fast,
And so does the world's climate.
When we pollute the sea,
We destroy the Earth.
We are making animals and plants extinct,
When we should be protecting them.
We ruin habitats such as rainforests;
We don't help them, we ruin them.
Just think of the future:
Everyone can play a part
Just by not using plastic.
Nature would be saved if we recycled and use renewable sources,
So let's work together to save the environment!

Reyha Rahman (10)
Whitehall Junior Community School, Walsall

The Polar Bears And Global Warming

Polar bears live in misery
That puts tears in me
And breaks little bits of me.
Their homes melt when global warming hits -
That's when the world isn't fixed.
I know these words are jumbled and mixed,
But all I'm trying to say is
Let these polar bears live
In a world where there is peace and hope.
So please say *nope*
To global warming,
And wake up the next morning
To realise you had made a change.

Humera Sayf (11)
Whitehall Junior Community School, Walsall

Global Warming

Temperatures are increasing,
Like our seas are emptying.
Our glaciers melt:
Tip, tip.
You can hear the glaciers fading away.
No more clear air,
Just carbon dioxide,
A drop of scarce loved rain.
A million trees would be appreciated.
The climate is unpredictable,
Boiling heat is everywhere.
Although it is not too late;
We can save the Earth,
There is still hope.
We can do it -
You can too.

Laiba Chaudhry (11)
Whitehall Junior Community School, Walsall

Have You Ever Wondered…?

Have you ever wondered
Why the sky is blue?
Have you ever wondered
Why our grass is so green?
Have you ever wondered
Why water runs cold and clear?
Blue skies turn to grey and then
Where will the children play?
The green grass can turn to brown,
Making smiles turn to frowns.
Water could stop running clear,
Then people would shed a tear.
Have you ever wondered?
I have,
Have *you*?

Aleena Zaynab (10)
Whitehall Junior Community School, Walsall

Tree Of Life

The one and only tree of life is very bright,
With dancing leaves and flowers that are white.

The long and huge tree of life has might:
Whatever comes, wood choppers or fires, it still remains with might.

Oh, save the tree, for it is part of Earth;
Trees absorb carbon dioxide, you should know what it's worth.

And in the end, whatever comes,
The one and only tree of life will be left standing.

Anureet Sidhu (10)
Whitehall Junior Community School, Walsall

Our Planet!

How could we betray the Earth?
We're the Earth and the Earth is us.
Every tree,
And every bee:
Personally, I feel like humans are trying to flee.
We really need this to discuss,
People don't believe our time is running
And lots of people are doing nothing.
We really need to rush -
This can be blamed on us.
Please listen to this message:
If you don't it will cause a wreckage.

Nikola Seferyn (11)
Whitehall Junior Community School, Walsall

What Will Earth Be?

Days go by,
Bad things are happening;
People are trashing,
The turtles are dying.

You throw trash in the ocean,
And then the whales see.
Then you realise
It was me.

Use paper bags,
Use paper straws,
To save the sea
And imagine what it could be...

Help the animals,
Clean the sea,
Because one day you will say:
What will the Earth be...?

Maimoona Sajjad (10)
Whitehall Junior Community School, Walsall

There I Lie

There I lie,
Hoping not to get trashed on.
There I lie,
Wishing the chaos was gone.
There I lie,
Praying for a peaceful day.
There I lie,
Waiting for the rubbish monster to go away.
There I lie,
Staying still in fear.
There I lie,
Wishing I was not here.
There I lie,
Seeing the bottles and bags being thrown.
There I lie,
Thinking: *why is this my home?*

Qaylah Esakjee (10)
Whitehall Junior Community School, Walsall

Climate Change

Climate change may be frightening,
So to save the planet we need to start recycling.
Fossil fuels are burning -
One day this will make the world stop turning.

Fires, hurricanes, and droughts;
We need to sort this out!
Our Earth is melting,
We are not helping.

Nothing is unchangeable;
This problem is changeable.
Everyone is capable -
I hope this poem is persuadable.

Sofia Mohammed (10)
Whitehall Junior Community School, Walsall

Take Care Of Our Climate

Everything is changing,
The world is full of pollution.
It just feels wrong;
No one is taking care of it.

We've lived many years,
And still it's full of rubbish.
We need to take care of the Earth -
We don't want the climate to change.
Please take care of our world... please!

Najiha Awal (7)
Whitehall Junior Community School, Walsall

Earth

E veryone can help save the Earth
A nd make it better by working together
R ainforest's trees need to stop being chopped down
T ogether we can achieve more
H over around and let's start by putting the right material in the right bin.

Zaina Hussain (11)
Whitehall Junior Community School, Walsall

YOUNG WRITERS INFORMATION

We hope you have enjoyed reading this book – and that you will continue to in the coming years.

If you're the parent or family member of an enthusiastic poet or story writer, do visit our website **www.youngwriters.co.uk/subscribe** and sign up to receive news, competitions, writing challenges and tips, activities and much, much more! There's lots to keep budding writers motivated!

If you would like to order further copies of this book, or any of our other titles, then please give us a call or order via your online account.

Young Writers
Remus House
Coltsfoot Drive
Peterborough
PE2 9BF
(01733) 890066
info@youngwriters.co.uk

**Join in the conversation!
Tips, news, giveaways and much more!**

YoungWritersUK YoungWritersCW youngwriterscw

Scan me to watch The Big Green video!